INSTRUCTIONS OF THE SPIRIT

poems & intimations

by

D. Patrick Miller

Fearless Books ✻ Berkeley, California

Fearless Books
2342 Shattuck Avenue #506
Berkeley CA 94704 • *www.fearlessbooks.com*

Publisher's Cataloging-in-Publication
(Provided by Quality Books, Inc.)

Miller, D. Patrick, 1953-
  Instructions of the spirit : poems & intimations / by
D. Patrick Miller.
  p. cm.
  ISBN 0-9656809-6-7

  1. Spiritual life—Poetry.   I. Title.
PS3613.I535I68 2004   811'.6
                          QB133-2045

Some of these poems have previously appeared in *The Sun,*
Yellow Silk, Berkeley Poetry Review, Presumptions: A Letter at Large
and two collections: *1984 Anthology of Magazine Verse & Yearbook
of American Poetry* (Monitor Books) and *Changing Light: Eternal
Cycle of Night and Day* (HarperCollins, 1992)

CONTENTS

INTRODUCTION, 1
i can't shake the moonies, 5
August, 6
The Bandit, 8
The Belladonna Holds A Captive, 10
Pelicanidae, 11
Prize from the Sea, 13
Dream of the SheBear, 14
Early Darkness, 16
List for a Long Night, 17
"the warmth of real objectivity," 19
Sonnet for Swimmers, 21

Visiting North Carolina, 23-27
I THE BRIDGE, 24
II SAVING AND WASTE, 25
III THE NAMES, 26

Barefoot, 28
List for a Bad Mood, 30
On Sleeplessness, 31
After Pain, 34
A Birthday Tanka, 35
Lullaby, 36

The Geography of Illness, 37
Someone is Restless in the Kitchen, 38
Homunculus, 40
My God, 42
Odyssey, 44
The Fall, 45
Reversals, 46
Adjustment, 47
Projection, 48
Instructions of the Spirit, 50
Uncertainty Principle, 51
Aftershocks, 53
Bardo, 54
Perfect Happiness, 55
What the Meek Shall Do, 56
Ablaze, 57

"*Like the burlesk comedian,
I am abnormally fond of that precision
which creates movement.*"

— e.e. cummings

INTRODUCTION

A GOOD POEM is a newborn: compact, energetic, and full of potential. It appears in the world as if by magic, and is not far removed from the formless realm of spirit. Like an infant, a poem should grow on you, revealing more of its character and personality as time goes by. And the surprise of what it may become is usually not apparent at its birth.

When I recently titled a poem "Instructions of the Spirit," I suddenly recognized the role that poetry has played in my life as a writer. For me a poem arises from a mystical instinct, as if Somebody Up There (or In There?) is trying to tell me something, and it's my job to figure out what it is and get it down on the page. But as I mentioned, spirit is *formless* and so its communications consist of hunches, ah-ha's, oomphs, and bumps in the night. It's not that spirit speaks in code, because it doesn't have a language. In fact I'm the one who's writing in a kind of code: a translation of the ineffable. Whether I write good code or useless code is really up to the reader to determine. All I can do is pay attention to the input and carefully craft the output.

Although I've never been prolific as a poet – this collection represents most of the poems I consider printable that I wrote from age twenty to fifty – I've always considered poetry to be the "root work" of all the other writing I've done, from journalism to fiction to essays, even advertising and public relations. Poetry is at the core of my writing because it is both the most instinctive of all the scribbler's forms and the hardest to refine. Even though most poems seem to write themselves at first, I sometimes find myself tinkering with the words decades after I thought they were finished. This is another way in which poems are like children: they have their own life but the author can influence their maturing over the years.

The poems are followed by remarks and reflections that I call "intimations." These brief asides are not attempts to explain the poems, because anyone who's ever sat through Poetry Appreciation 101 knows that explanation can kill a poem right off. But I do try to provide a few intimate glimpses into where poems have come from or where they might be going, much as I would do at a public reading. Since I can't give readings everywhere this book goes, these intimations are my stand-ins for a personal appearance. I also hope that these asides encourage the reader to take another look at each poem, because any good poem usually requires a second reading to get acquainted with it. The baby who at first seems to be speaking gibberish may actually be giving voice to a revealing code.

The poems here are arranged in a rough chronological order. Some of the early ones seem "young" to me in retrospect, without as much precision as I would like a poem to have now. But my discretion in choosing work for this volume relied less on determining technical competence than instinctive content; I asked myself if each poem conveyed some of the spark that made me write it down. If so, the poem made the grade for this collection. My aim is to share as many of those sparks as I can, so that the reader may more readily understand the hunches, ah-ha's, oomphs, and bumps in the night that spirit provides to us all. Because, oddly enough, it's our ability to translate such weird and mysterious instructions from beyond the pale that makes life make sense.

Instructions of the Spirit

i can't shake the moonies

they are on to me on sidewalks
   transit platforms
   and in the library
they are always asking me to
   dinner with many moonies:
won't i come float in the chasm of loss
   with them?
won't i revive the infant
   disciplined within me?
don't i want to keep
   bewilderment at bay?

when i tell the hundredth one no
he is more assured than the others.
he says "it's all right.
   you must be a chosen one."

great; just my luck

Growing up in the South where I was asked too often if I had accepted Jesus Christ as my personal savior, I was happy to think I had escaped evangelism when I reached the streets of San Francisco at age 22. Instead I seemed to become a magnet for religious salespeople of a different stripe. Looking back, I'm intrigued to recognize how spiritual experience wore its most annoying disguise at a time when I considered myself too intelligent for religion of any sort. I guess the signs were indicating that this aspect of my life just wasn't going to go away.

August

From the crackling brown, littered
field of fallow walks a crazy maiden.
She's been leaping from log to log
in a ritual of secret celebration, and
her face is wet, even her long breasts
are sweating, her shirt thrown somewhere
in the weeds. Her burnt cheeks are not smooth,
her black eyes are not gentle, and her feet
are like leather from so many escapes
into the rough.
She is worried by what she may have
forgotten, and what might lie ahead
beyond her control.
Perhaps tomorrow the field will be
leveled by a runway, her jumping-logs
buried in driven earth,
the dry aroma of the tall grass
overpowered by fuel oil and tarmac.
Then she would borrow money she
could not repay, to fly to the tropics
and learn how to live in a
rainforest. She has seen a movie
about this. *She could do it.*

———————

Some people are born into a wilder species than the rest of us, their nature a step or two closer to pure animal instinct. Clothing never really suits them and conventional lifestyles are out of the question. These human creatures are always a reminder that spirit drives all levels of being, and is not necessarily interested in fomenting civilization as we know it.

The Bandit

Even among this maze of lighted houses
Arises the disorderly smell of raccoon:
    the bandit,
    the fierce organizer,
    one-who-walks-in-a-huddle.
They come down from the dry hills
By who knows what paths –
    surely not along the road –
Come to overturn garbage
And seethe at the dull and domestic:
    dogs, cats,
    people's toys.
They freeze in the sudden light
And growl with a body improbably deep.

Late in the night
They and their energetic children
    root and roust beneath your house
As if building a place of their own
Down there. Their tricky hands
    turn out halfhuman noises
    which time and time again
Poke cleanly through your dreams.

Embedded within our consciousness is the silent history of other creatures, older ways of seeing, and natural environments unaltered by human influences. Evolution and technical progress have changed us from neighbors to invaders everywhere we live, but sometimes other creatures turn the tables on us. They "move in" not just on our real estate, but on our awareness as well – challenging us to recall all that we've seen through other eyes, sensed with different antennae, and understood before we knew language.

The Belladonna Holds A Captive

This complicated flower,
    growing once and twice from its beginning,
    curling into white waxed peaks
        holds a secret sunk and rooted by its organs.
A terrible bodyless beast is snared inside,
    refused form or evolution
    by some ancient decision of grace.
A snarl that could have frozen hearts
is wrapped in silence, deep in green sheathing...

The venom of the beast is the fragrance of the flower.
When we enter the room,
    we find the air painted with sweet rancor.

———————

Admittedly, we tend to see ourselves in the world around us, but how often are we seeing more than we know about ourselves? When I studied this flower, I had the strong intuition that it could have manifested in a different form with the same root energy. I didn't know it at the time, but I was sensing an important truth of the spiritual path: We have the capacity to shapeshift with our own consciousness, turning the brutality of the unbridled ego into something like a "sweet rancor." The point of spiritual growth is not to achieve an unalloyed goodness, but to find the full depth and complexity of our power.

Pelicanidae

Somewhere a crescent of fishermen
advance in shallow waters,
forcing confusion below them,
selecting what they will from
random flashes of panic

but the singular flyer I know
rests in a tuck on a white rock island
amid a warm blue sky and
the chill, bluer sea.
In cooling repose it bleeds salt
and air, the flat eyes of alacrity
betraying naught but a windy silence.
The still collection of subtle,
scattered hints from the listing world
mounts until
a sudden trigger to flight
unhinges the arms of feather & bone
to climb upon the long, broad ribbon
of the free hunt, a swift,
measured wheeling over the far currents

which yield life to the quick
and murmur the rhythm of return.

What if birds are the most spiritually advanced of all mortal beings, having honed their bodies down to little more than weightless feathers and hollow bones? I've dreamt of flying in precise maneuvers, as if I have an instinctive knowledge I can't use in my present shape and form. Am I recalling a pterodactyl lifetime, or anticipating a freewheeling way of life yet to come?

Prize from the Sea

A boy holds a small body, completely given
on his palm, its mouth and fan ends
both turning down, learning gravity.
He presents his spoiling trophy
to the sunshine, the cellular gleam
of its whiteness not yet faded, but drying,
dulling — light following life loosed
in the capture.

The boy is proud now.
He was a little frightened by the
animal's acrobatics of yielding,
the wild arcs and wet slamming,
its reflexive dance into the fatal
discomfort of the great beyond.

It breathed in water.
It slept in the currents.

---

*Death is always a rude shock, especially when we first learn that we have
a hand in it — and then again, when we recognize that death will eventually
lay a hand upon us. Spiritual maturity arrives with the realization that the
life and death of the body are not all that matter. In fact that realization is
where we turn the corner from living a life dictated by fear and greed to a
life imbued with originality and generosity.*

Dream of the SheBear

Somehow I thought you had come home unannounced,
creeping early, soft and naked from the airport,
slipping into bed behind me,
luggage abandoned on the circling carousel.
I decided to pretend sleeping a few moments longer.

But your surprise was more complex, for I felt
your spoonshape embrace enlarging around me.
Soon you were ten feet tall, and your clasp
bestowed the forbidden power of animal wildness.
A shebear! I thought, and the world behind me
turned dark, fragrant, and slick with
all-night rain before a clearing dawn.
A moment longer I listened to waking songs
of the crickets, the birds, and the
unnameable things —

and then I turned to pounce, but instantly
you shifted into deer intelligence,
a four-legged, springing ballerina.
My opening eyes glimpsed only your last bound
over night's receding edge, as you raced to stay
within a world safe from human travelers.

The experience of dreams suggests that we live more lives than our daily one. Our present form may be a composite of former shapes, dimly remembered instincts, and ancient yearnings. When we sleep together we mingle realms of natural history.

Early Darkness

Think of it as ink:
an indigo dye descending
between the leaves of the trees
and down to the grasses.

There is no dying of the light —
just the washing of a bowl,
and overturning it for night.

When day arrives we must write with
        bottled darkness.
In the night we can dream
        free messages of light.

———————

An artist friend was a little depressed about the advent of long nights in the winter, so I tried to reinterpret the circumstances for her. This poem is also about how light and dark always contain each other: Our dreams can be full of light in the midst of darkness, while much of our unconscious fades to black in the daytime. When we write, we use little squiggles of black to bring what is hidden back to light.

List for a Long Night

There is a part of the brain
    that knows only faces;
there is a pattern for my hand
    that follows your face only:
        quiet eyes, skin warm and light,
         the upward arching mouth and
         fine hair of stilled phrases.
    All around your moonlike radiance
there is the darkness.

There are confessions, slow tears,
    names, stories, and our
    deep, torn trust...

There is soft rocking giving sighs
    and touches brief and restrained.
There are cautious lips meeting
    to bring together the air

    we breathe:
the hours are silent.
        There is the light

A young romance was my first introduction to spiritual devotion, although I didn't recognize it as such at the time. What I did know was that this relationship required a continuing inner dedication even after its intimate phase was over. This poem marked the first step in years of healing. It's the brief chronicle of a reunion – a word that aptly describes everyone's spiritual destination.

"the warmth of real objectivity"

Here is
the surprise of the moon,
stepping down from blue gleaming
to bear close upon the blood
with miraculous intent:

A lost face hunting
tears of recognition,
night limbs seeking
the root of an old embrace,
cold, far voices sounding
the harmonies risen from
light falling through the ocean.

When the earth shifts
time opens in the water,
the sky fractures and
the human eye closes
    to a kiss,
a worldly eye opens to
    the whisper
of the tide drowning in the sand.

A long time ago this poem wrote itself with minimal intervention from my intellect. Every once in a while it's good to say things that need to be said without understanding what they mean. But I comprehend much more of this poem with twenty years or so of retrospect: it was one of my first glimpses into a world of mystical experience, something I was distant from in my youth when I was so focused on changing the everyday world as a budding journalist. The title is a wonderful phrase by philosopher Jacob Needleman from his book The Heart of Philosophy.

Sonnet for Swimmers

Rain falls through an open heart
to cool my addled world of *maya*
with tears from the sea of remembering;
A wind of lights passes softly
in the deep night of dreaming, and
draws the eyes of the drifters there;
A dancer pauses in her garden's dark soil
and is entered by a new desire.

When a breath of certain strength
is loosened, and reaches for the length
and depth and broad way of water,
Then the magic body surpasses
the striving of the visible limbs,
Turning swiftly, as no thought can turn.

The "magic body" of the spirit is seldom entirely comfortable in the physical body and the state of mind where we attempt to hold it captive. In young adulthood we experience a kind of wrestling match between our conscious self and the much more deeply rooted spiritual self; many of our best-laid plans can go awry because we are not following a clear motivation from deep within. Eventually the spirit strikes out in a new direction, seeking for us a way of life somehow more authentic than what we have yet found, and dares us to follow.

Visiting North Carolina, June 1984

This cycle of three prose poems was written soon after a trip home to my birthplace, about seven years after I had moved to California, and shortly before I became seriously ill for a period of seven years. Southerners have a hard time pulling up roots. Although these poems may seem to reaffirm my roots, they actually helped me recognize home as a state of mind rather than a geographical location. Letting go of some sentimental attachments was the first step toward an inevitable crisis of healing.

I THE BRIDGE

When we were children
we would meet by the bridge;
you would take a folded paper
from your pocket and give it to me:
a poem, or a song lyric you loved.
I was excited by the paper; it was warm,
and wrinkled by your curves. As I read it
you would blink and smile. Under the bridge
we would talk for an hour, and stand together
in the creek, kissing, cold water and sand
washing our ankles, our feet slowly sinking.
When we were children, the secrecy of kissing
was everything — a new world began there,
for we had never been in love before.

Now the years have nearly doubled
and we spend our first night as lovers.
We call the children, and they are here,
whispering, while two strangers explore
the deliberate excitement of adults.
Your hair, still long and wild, is gray,
which stirs and fascinates me.
Later, as you sleep, I hold and watch you,
my arm across your breasts, and I am content.
This is a rare happiness: the readiness
for dying that makes sense of life.
The children are let go, and in your sleep
you smile at their perfection.

II SAVING AND WASTE

Outside my grandmother's house,
now empty and simple, I help my parents
pull gray oaken boards from the shed
my grandfather built. My father uses the wood
for picture frames, and gives his brothers & sisters
photographs of the house. The wood is sixty years
old, solid, strong, and "never dressed,"
my father says.

He pulls the boards loose from one end,
and my mother holds them out while he crowbars
loose the center nails, then the other end.
On the ground I hammer the nails out by their points,
then flip the board and pull them out.
Most of them are loose, pulling out by hand,
their passage smoothed by rust gone to powder.
A few are difficult even with a claw hammer,
resisting the undoing of work done well
so long ago. I toss them all into the shed
— now becoming a skeleton —
onto a pile of other wood, broken tools and
things that will never be of use again.
I think about how much we waste,
how much we save,
and whether my grandfather could have guessed
the further use of what he built. My father
walks to the back of the shed, crowbar in hand,
and stops for a moment, his mouth slightly open,

for he is slightly surprised. The back wall
has many gaps; someone — his brother? —
has been here, and some of the finest boards
are already gone.

III   THE NAMES

We ride through my mother's country,
and my father's: I see the steps where
my mother sat and talked after class in
high school, 45 years ago. I'm shown the
intersection where my father had a flat tire,
and left the car to hitch-hike to his wedding.
"It was easier back then," says my mother,
"and of course he was in uniform."

This is a country now of churches and
hunters, Thursday night bingo, alcoholism,
poverty, fast food, and family gardens.
There is what city people call a closeness
to the earth, and there is meanness and
bigotry. There is common sense, and a
sense of plainness in living day to day.
There is a bizarre growth of satellite dishes,
and new, wider highways pulsing nervously
with the traffic of rapid change.

My parents left this country
to make themselves over, near the city.
I left it all, floating, balloon-like,
to another side of the continent, but
riding through here I realize, with mixed relief,
that my tether has not been cut.
There is meanness, bingo, deprivation,
and red clay in my very blood,
and these toughen my stubborn heart.

We drive through a quadrant of Lutheran churches
and a wide plaza of tombstones on either side
of the road. I read the names of my family,
and their kin, friends, lovers & enemies
for generations: Eckard, Bowman, Fry, Miller,
Killian, Yount, and Campbell. The same names
appear again and again. Suddenly I feel the
tether tied right here, rooted at the level
of death, and through it I hear the muttering
of these names, and all the questions left
on the lips of the puzzled and persistent.

Barefoot

The earth is my masseuse.
Her sticks and stones are not my bones,
but her points are therapeutic.

If talking were walking,
we'd all be home by now. Six ways
lead to heaven, where silence rains.

You can get there from here.
Take two lefts when you feel it's right,
and wait there. Someone will know you.

The path follows water.
Green fronds slap at my ankles, small
fishes panic at my footsteps.

The planet turns, soaked through
with warmth and melodrama. No
overseer, no fence, no slaves.

Extraterrestrials
feign disinterest. The skies flash
with the reds and greens of traffic.

This poem was written soon after I became seriously ill at age 32 from an auto-immune collapse that would eventually lead to a full-blown spiritual crisis spanning seven years. Accustomed to feeling healed by nature when I was a child, I took a walk around a lake, barefoot, to try to regain some of my lost connection. It didn't work. Instead I began to realize that there was no turning back to earlier ways of being. Something was up; the skies were flashing.

List for a Bad Mood

the mudflow, stopping
an iron bar sinking
the grey stone buried
a fossil cracked by a hammer
a thought never opened
a bone without a body
six quiet memories contained in one grief
a wheel, a planet, a dropping bell
small animals watching the moon
rain gathering in a sliver of the sky
children with nothing to say, walking
a river with nowhere to go
the simple principle of fog
an old building, burned, waiting
nothing given, nothing gained
a white wall, stucco
leaves from the ocean
action or inaction
sorrow

----

*I read somewhere that if you don't know how to start a poem, start
a list and go from there. What you choose to catalogue at any particular
moment will be as much an inventory of your mind as an enumeration of
the things you happen to see around you. We don't really see the world as
it is; we select a version of creation that reaffirms our assumptions and
reflects our emotions of the moment.*

On Sleeplessness *(for my mother)*

Very early, your heart burst open
like an overstuffed suitcase, and the clothes,
jewelry, well-worn dolls, watches, crutches
and cameos of your ancestors spilled inside you.
Your soul was draped with grief before
you could speak, and no one could see
that your first lullaby should be a threnody.
The unhappy dead are petulant beings,
peering through the eyes of their living kin
to glimpse the light at the end of the tunnel.
No one told you who their voices were,
and why they murmured of so much bitterness
and fear. No one taught you that
the lost ones need first to be heard,
then forgiven and released.

                                        And so, drawn
by your strength and independence, these spirits
rushed in through your broken heart like
a river flooding the breach of a dam.
They took back the clothes and jewelry,
putting on whatever they found at random,
shoving and fighting each other to try on
precious things that might prettify their misery.
Feeding on the life that should have been yours
alone, these desperate souls of many disguises
then possessed you. It is they who,

unable to rest, have stolen your sleep
for so many years.

You know, they thought
I was an open door as well. Lately they
have brought their morbid partying
into my stomach and my dreams –
but when I awaken in the night, I *know* them.
Not their names or faces, but their truths
and traumas: Someone starved. Someone
was born dead and, like a turtle trapped
on its back, struggled to move in a useless body
and silence the screams of his terrified mother.
Someone murdered, someone was slain, a father
ignored and abused his daughters with an anger
he inherited. I recognize a family, like any
human group, with a legacy of pain and
unspoken longing. And by watching you
I have learned their desire...

I can bring them
peace, but they must give up thieving
the sleep of the living. I am the poet
and the storyteller, their voice and
their master. I will honor them,

but I will put them to rest.

Diagnosed as manic-depressive before "bipolar" became the fashionable term, my mother always seemed to be struggling against a dark and overwhelming psychic inheritance. After coming out of a coma following a near-successful suicide attempt, she told me in whispers that she had felt "someone leave my body" – someone who had always been there without her knowledge or permission. When my illness struck me at the same age she had first become ill, with many of the same physical symptoms that she suffered before her psychiatric diagnosis was made, I recognized our common inheritance.

After Pain

Forgiving is a night spring,
a sparkling ribbon of release
spilling from the heart to the sea
of nourishment. The late, low moon
flashes on the stream's surface.
Sleep quietly and feel yourself
carried by the water's gravity
of ceaseless return.

As soon as you arise,
a young horse prancing at the dawn
finds his strength and leaps the gate
on his first try. Walk through
the wet grass to find him.
He'll be standing in the new light,
near the joining of the waters,
where the sorrow you have yielded
weds the river of wakefulness.

———————

Much of my illness centered around severe symptoms rooted in my abdomen, the "sea of nourishment" in traditional Chinese medical terminology. I had to forgive a thousand angers and let the healing energy make its internal transit from heart to stomach, again and again, in order to heal. I have few poems from this very intense period, but occasionally a dream simply wrote itself out.

A Birthday Tanka

While I sort through words
for my mother's seventy
circles round the sun
the rain returns softly, peace
slowly soaking the night soil.

---

*The tanka is a traditional Japanese poetic form predating the haiku.
It is arranged in five lines with a syllable count of 5-7-5-7-7. Like haiku,
a tanka focuses on an image of nature, but it also reveals the poet's relat-
ionship to that image. This was my gift to my mother when she was seventy.
Two years later she surprised everyone and passed away peacefully in her
sleep. Who knows what factors contribute to such a transit, but I was glad
we had largely let go of our grievances.*

Lullaby

I am not a body. I am the rain,
falling all over your house and
in the deep fold of the distant hills.
I cover the leaf, the roof, the field grasses
and the shiny street. A billowing wind
carries me through the swirling branches
and drives me against your window.
I strike and coalesce, fall and spill
into the soil and the swallowing gutter,
taking a wild ride to the sea.
Later the sun will draw me up,
but the clouds will lose me when
they let down their burden in water
again. I am not a body. You can
sleep to the sound of my falling.

———————————

Part of the process of spiritual surrender is learning to release our own consciousness into the watery medium of the spirit. Instead of anxiously planning what should happen to us next, we learn to "go with the flow." Instead of trying to make ourselves different, better, or higher than the rest of creation, we learn to be content with the sensations of falling, soaking through, and cycling between different states of being. Science tells us that our bodies are mostly water; spirituality teaches us how to live that truth.

M

FELLOWSHIP FOR TODAY
LIBRARY CHECK OUT CARD

You are preparing a permanent record for our library, so please print or write legibly.

Title Instructions of the Spirit

Author (Last, First) D. Patrick Miller

☑ Book   ☐ CD/Tape   ☐ DVD/Video

☐ Other (Please specify): _____

Category MP

To check out this library book / item, remove this check out card from the library book / item then, on the back of this card, enter your name, phone number & check out date and place it in the Library check out box.

Full Name - Phone	Check Out Date

The Geography of Illness   *for Laurie*

The night world clamors with change, the moans
of the dying competing with the shrieks of the birthing
like tuneless karaoke spirits in an otherworld bar.
Windwrapped trees gesture like public speakers
and the murky meadow stream sings like a canary,
telling everyone everything. The very ground toils
with its troubles, and bubbles and bubbles.
Faults are shifting and continents drifting; the whole
body's earth is alive with intrigue and impossibilities.

Welcome to the party of the strange and nearly-ready!
This world will be raising hell until the slow sun,
still nodding off beyond the horizon, awakens
to cast a nourishing beam on something utterly new,
rising slenderly between plowed soil and a solid stone —
a thing so lovely it's fierce, a no-nonsense blossom,
this very wild flower with a backbone.

---

*There are certain illnesses that are shamanic in nature, meaning they tear
apart one's old way of being in order to let a new way assert itself. You
can't see these spiritual revolutions coming, and for a long time they seem
to have delivered nothing more than a painful anarchy. Like lightning, spirit
seeks a conductor — and it doesn't hesitate to singe your hair and fry your
circuits while delivering the kind of jolt you think you can't handle. But
you can, if just barely.*

37

Someone is Restless in the Kitchen

A soft old drunk
fusses in the darkened pantry,
repeating names,
gesturing for emphasis.

He is obsessed with eating,
searching for the special treat
missed by everyone
in the convivial gathering
of hours before.

I enter the kitchen and catch his eye,
but he sees I am a dream.
Unperturbed, he opens all the small doors
and rattles the dishes, crinkles plastic
wrappings, knocks silverware
to the floor.

He's acting like a blind man,
but he is simply wise and reckless.

There's an old saying that suggests "when the student is ready the teacher will appear." The spiritual teacher can be another person or an inner fount of previously hidden wisdom; either way the teacher is a troublemaker, determined to upset the apple cart of our habitual perceptions and most prized assumptions about reality. Left to our own devices, we can make such a mess of life that it's the messenger of love & truth who looks demented. That's why it may take a few missed opportunities before we've developed the humility and open-mindedness to recognize the perfect stranger.

Homunculus

Christ the lost man is stepping bone to bone
through the dark cavern where our heart is hiding.

He searches deep in the body
where bitterness gives root to fear,
where habit buries the stirrings of change
like stones of the colossus smothering the grass,
where the cells of original virtue
swim unknown among cancers.

He tires:
the air in here is old and full of war.
He strains to hear the outside world
coming in through the holes in the head
and catches an echo of television.
He longs for a place of rest
where he might await heroism —
then smiles at his forgetfulness.
Long ago the mind diffused him into the blood,
that he might be celebrated for the hemorrhage to follow.
Such was the honor of crucifixion.

Now from the dim inside
he pushes mightily on the low rib
with the patience of humility, an austere musicianship,
hoping again to start a magic expansion,
each rib following each upward

in a subtle loosening toward a great song,
a rhythmic, passionate massage of space
yielding the heart room to rise
and birth from its singularity
the thousand dense and brilliant inventions
of love
of which we dream through Christ.

———— · • ————

Homunculus is a Latin word meaning "little man," alluding to the ancient notion that human consciousness is directed by a tiny interior being, like an imp or fairy who keeps an apartment in our minds. Quite apart from the historical figure of Jesus, I often think of the Christ as just such an internal operator, a secret agent for love and wisdom who has a devil of a time just getting our attention.

My God

I believe in an ex-God, relieved of omnipotence
for His inconstancy and poor management decisions.
His trouble began with that business over His only
begotten Son. After eons of simply smoting the unrighteous,
my God sacrificed His lone hippie offspring in a futile attempt
to shame humanity into doing the right thing.
The tactic was unprecedented, the timing unwise.

What could have been a great executive dynasty
thus died in disrepute. God had to leave the beings made
in His own image to the chaos of natural disasters
and capitalism triumphant. Father and Son never reconciled;
now the Christ wanders the galaxies as a New Age therapist,
still bitter about being forsook, lending aid and comfort
to alien whores and beggars, his earthly habits unrefined.

My God finally opened a café on the celestial Seine
where He succors lost souls who starved for want of dominion
on His lost planet. So now He whiles away eternity at a
sidewalk table playing monopoly with the disfavored dead:
tinhorn dictators, tyrannical moms,
     power addicts of every description.
He has grown a fat belly and is too fond of fresh madeleines
and kir. My God is a mess, I confess, but our bond transcends
all fate and folly: I still believe in Him
                    because He still believes in Me.

Almost every religion has conferred the dubious gift of personhood upon God so that we could assume it was God who conferred personhood upon us. Then it's a short step to believing that God's person resembles ours, and pretty soon you have the basis for deadly wars of religion. This poem is my sacreligious anthem to a very personal God, mercifully retired if not entirely out of commission.

Odyssey

It's good to be home. The long pulling over great water
has brought our ships within view of the lonely, azure sound
from whence we set forth so long ago, seeking our fortune,
trailing the dawn on a race into the sea. We have learned
that nothing is as it seems: The bright sun never does set
and the earth is not solid, its core still brewing with the
same feverish chaos that birthed all the farflung planets
and set the blue sky spinning on the fingertip of God.

Now we've returned to shock our kinfolk with the tattered rags
of our once-fine clothing, the skulls of slower enemies,
and intoxicating powders ground by naked strangers.
We reek like beasts, yet a new civilization is in
our hold: like an Ark we have gathered all the world's visions,
two by two, and soon we will loose them on familiar shores.

---

*There was a time when the greatest human explorations ventured into the
earth's unknown territories. Now that we have broken all the globe's frontiers
and find space travel slowed by great dangers and distances, we are beginning
to face the inner frontiers of consciousness – and sensing that our own visions
may provide the keys to unlocking universal mysteries.*

The Fall

There is a long fall from the perch of habitual pain.
The ocean below looks like glass, a sunlit mirror
that promises a shattering end to the driven world
of winning, losing, wanting and getting. We played the game
and lost our shirts; we faced the demons within and without
but lost our nerve at the last minute. Now we make a wind
just by dropping through the air; we make a teapot's whistle
by the speed of our descent, an accelerating sigh.

We *worked* for this grand fall — not for the earth to rush at us!
Not this conspiracy of gravity with the mad lunge
of the galaxy racing to nowhere in record time.
Our leisurely surrender has been cut off by God,
the crazed planet-thrower who taunts us now to pull up short
and choose joy at last, dancing all the way home on water.

---

*Although I've never been suicidal, I've always been intrigued by the parallels
of self-murder and ego death. One is a final act of self-absorption, the other
a painful but necessary step along the spiritual path. The ego can die a
thousand times and yet find ways to resurrect itself, only to head inexorably
in the direction of destruction once again. Getting off the melodramatic
morbid-go-round of the ego doesn't require destroying ourselves, just learning
how to go through this life a little more light-footed.*

Reversals

The dry winds of autumn have invaded spring, uprooting
trees and expectations and bringing power to the ground.
The ancient snake is made young again, and beasts of the night
are seen standing on bright sidewalks, blinking at the sunlight.
The police are not arresting; their tear-stung eyes cannot
focus on crime. Killers on the loose flock to the green sea
to breathe their last, drowning in the mercy of deep sorrow
flushed to the surface and sent crashing onto stony shores.

On such a day of reversals, wisdom walks in plain sight,
stops for coffee and a croissant at the corner café
and listens intently to the insensible chatter
of a dirty vagabond who lost her way in the dark.
The winds will shift back tomorrow, and wisdom seeks a form
to fill when appearances deceive. Anyone will do.

---

*Sometimes you have a really strange day, when the veils of perception seem
especially translucent and a barely contained reality, entirely different from
what you're accustomed to, seems about to break through. The fact that things
soon return to "normal" is either a blessing or a curse, depending on how you
look at it. As A Course in Miracles suggests, "Enlightenment is a recognition,
and not a change at all."*

Adjustment

It is the subtle tightening at the root of one bright spoke
that will true the wheel and end the wobbling uncertainty
of our ride toward home. The wind has not unsettled us,
nor the uneven roadway, nor the distraction of night
falling around us like a spell cast by mischievous gods.
No, it was the unseen loosening of but one thin bone,
disrupting the symphony of all the bones protecting
our spinning heart, that set us wavering on this long path.

Now here is the simple test of our long, complicated life:
Can we make a gentle correction in the right moment,
neither turning too far, nor shying away from the need
to turn this rib in its socket? We cannot know our skill
until we find ourselves at home, or drifting further,
but it is time to apply the precise tension of love.

---

*Here is a bicyclist's view of the spiritual path, inspired by my recent
realization that the two-wheeled journeys of my life have been my
chosen routes to altered states of consciousness. Like meditation, long-
distance cycling is a simple, repetitive effort pursued with a transfor-
mative intensity. When I tour by bike, the destination is secondary
to the focus and determination that this medium of travel demands.
And so it goes with the spiritual journey.*

Projection

This daylight is but a bright shade of darkness,
    a cascade of reflected shadows
flickering uncertainly like a decaying film,
painting the herky-jerky of human folly
in quaint sepia. We spy the present instantly
before it becomes ancient history, old fibers
of light peeling and flaking away in the vault
of sentiment. In our habit of memoriam,
we pine for what has passed and hope
that it will return in a shining future,
in a new light, reillumined – but that
is the cinematography of death, a trailer
of sad fantasy projected across the mind.
We have bought our tickets for a show
worth remembering, but we are looking for light
in a large dark room. We need to get up
and walk out, drop our timepieces and
vanish into the dazzling truth. That's life.

———— · · ————

Two months before his death in 1952, the spiritual teacher Paramahansa Yogananda, author of the famed Autobiography of a Yogi, said this to a gathering of his followers:

"This earth is nothing but movies to me... The first movie that I saw in India, I stayed there all night, for everything was tumbling and disappearing. And what a great fun I had that night! Somebody said, 'Why do you want to see the picture all night?' I said, 'I am seeing the big picture show... I am watching the big movie in the little movie.' And they then understood... I saw only shadows and light dancing. That's what happens to you when you know God."

Instructions of the Spirit

When dullness threatens, purify. Cut away
the resentments, suspicions, and petty fears
that have so long encroached on your good peace.
Savage your own sloth and torpor; show no
mercy to the motives that have so long purchased
only boredom, pride, and isolation. Convict
the warmaker within and execute without prejudice.
Murder your madness and leave no trace
        of the healing crime.

The gates of heaven lie just beyond this
battle for mastery — and only by winning
will you understand that it did not occur.
The devil who was never outside you was
never within, yet still you whisper gravely
of his insidious powers. Kill him now.
And stop retelling his poor stories!

---

*Excepting those who are hopelessly egocentric, most of us live in a
psychic borderland that can be called the "soul." This is where the
survival instincts and selfish motives we experience as individuals get
mixed up with the surpassing motivation of pure spirit, which doesn't
care whether we get what we want. We often don't want to hear what
the spirit has to say because it's not particularly "supportive" – although
it does compel us to work toward ultimate liberation. In my experience,
the voice of spirit is usually clear, uncompromising, and paradoxical.*

Uncertainty Principle

I'm just not so sure anymore. I don't know if
my mind extends beyond my nose but stops short
of yours. Through quantum spectacles, nothing quite
seems as if it is; I could be imagining all creation
or, hell, God could be playing dice with the cosmos.
There may be naught behind me but an unfurnished
vacuum, like an infinite convention hall with no
bookings, no trade fairs, no keynoters:
        just an air-conditioned silence forever killing time.
The wavery flashlight beam of my perception
could be leading me down a rathole, or straight
to a divine casino with all bets covered and
        an endless buffet!
That's how it goes this millennium: you're taking
Reality into your own hands just by walking
through the door you perceive every morning.
Newton and Descartes have been left for dead,
physicists roam the streets at will and
the universe is disappearing
        even as we stake our claims.

———————

Mystics and scientists have followed different routes to the same far destination: a full and final understanding of what makes the universe tick, where it came from and whether it has anywhere to go. Physicists have investigated ever smaller subdivisions of matter and energy; mystics have focused on the investigatory tool of consciousness itself. If you've paid any attention to the last century of discoveries in physics, you know that the most advanced science of matter is beginning to sound uncannily like the deepest mysticism of the mind.

Aftershocks

Gravity, my first crush! My shape unwittingly warped space
such that it answered with the mother of all attachments,
a force that would toss me down the stairs for a simple misstep
or hurl me from a buildingtop for an unwise moment
of melodramatic despair. You won't find another
lover quite so faithful, so willing to bring you down fast
to keep you from flying off the planet in a fancy
of star-dazzled freedom. This jealous mistress plays for keeps.

Sure, we fight; but who doesn't? I protest her clinginess
and she sends a shock through my faultlines, collapsing all
my stolid foundations. From the mad rubble of my ruins
I reconstruct a semblance of sanity, pleading for
peace and quiet, but she's already recharging her heart.

———————

Thanks to Brian Greene, author of The Elegant Universe, *for explaining
that the mysterious force of gravity is actually the result of how objects warp
space. I don't know about you, but to me that explains a lot.*

Bardo

I am spinning between this world and the next, circling through
exacting spirals, soaring above the bloodstained bunker
I built so long ago to defend my anger and keep
my heart from sending its subversive sentiments to my
righteous, overscheduled mind. I spin because I cannot
find a toehold among the cracked, well-worn tracks of my past
life, the one I was going through the motions of just the
other day, before all my bitter sorrow breathed its last.

It's crazy up here, where the air is too thin to think up
any good solid reasons to blame anyone for all
the mess down there, in the world I used to want, the earth where
I had carved a gravestone with the simplest of elegies:
"Here, lies..." Now, no more lies. I'm busted,
      cut loose from all ties to death,
launched in a new life, spun round by God's fierce fancy.

---

*At several critical turns in my life I've experienced attacks of vertigo, sustained
for days or weeks at a time, that seem to commemorate the passing of one way
of life and the arrival of another. I've always wondered what it might feel like
to reincarnate, and whether these dizzy spells are something like dress rehearsals.*

Perfect Happiness   *for Donald Trump*

I've coveted the moon, the stars, and sundry real estate
that I've seen taped across the picture window of my mind.
I've craved an infinite property of power and wealth,
my own sensual playground peopled by sly handmaidens
who could double as yes-men on a blue moment's notice.
When I was grasping, everything wouldn't have been too much
and I would have expected interest on the principle.
For more juice I'd have squeezed blood
     from the fat stone of the earth.

Now that my desiring is done, I'm left with nothing but
my birthday suit of space and time, shaky coordinates
that are falling out of fashion even as we ponder
where our next *raison d'etre* is coming from. Our will is
vanquished as science points the finger at a see-through God
Who wills for us a perfect happiness: the death of want.

---

*Of all the great spiritual imperatives, desirelessness may seem the hardest
to attain. The difficulty of giving up wanting makes one hope that we really
do experience multiple lifetimes with some learning potential that carries over
from one incarnation to the next. How else to finish all the steps of realiz-
ing that the happiness we instinctively seek is in none of the stuff we typi-
cally grasp for – and that the end of desire is not death, but the beginning
of really living?*

55

What the Meek Shall Do

Terror answers terror through history because so few
covet the slow, undramatic healing of peace and quiet.
All war begins with a bad habit: our long preference
for the fireworks of catastrophe, the lights and action
of plans exploding in chaos, good intentions gone wrong.
Better to be the harbingers of bitter mischief than
the guardians of ordinary goodwill: the money
is in death, the residuals flow from reruns of pain.

So pity the poor peacemakers who must sell duller goods:
no killing, no guts, no glory — not much of a story.
The news at six and eleven will mispronounce their names
if they are mentioned at all, and investors will not find
their meekness enticing. It's a hell of a business, this
mission to heal, this long ache of inheriting the earth.

———— · · ————

*I've always been astonished that our society glorifies its war dead and tends
to denigrate its peacemakers. After all, war is the same old story of human
fear and failure, while the effort to undo it — both within ourselves and in
the realm of geopolitics — requires an uncommon courage and consistency.*

Ablaze

There is a fire in the mirror: a slow conflagration
engulfs my form and lights my limbs with iridescent flame,
steadily consuming the bad blood of misadventures,
metabolizing the body's burden of old regrets,
converting the dead weight of sorrow into dancing light,
undoing the gravity of pain and allowing grace.
I am burning my forgetfulness: that artful daze which
has so long veiled the simple, loving choice of sanity.

When the smoke clears I will be a new man, cleaned by a blaze
of forgiveness that has taken down the walls of the mind
forever. The destruction of my city, my country,
my world and all my gods shall be complete, uncompromised,
and I will wander unchecked across all borders, lawless,
invisible, a joyful vagrant rudely setting fires.

———— · ————

Coming soon to your neighborhood!

D. PATRICK MILLER is a writer in Berkeley, California, who has published poetry, journalism, essays, and fiction in a wide variety of periodicals and authored six books, including one novel. After publishing several works with major houses, he founded Fearless Books in 1997 and created the online *Fearless Reviews*, an ongoing showcase of the best works from independent publishers. Besides this volume of poetry he is the author of "The Horse and the Wolf," a three-sonnet cycle of poems commemorating the tragedy of Sept. 11, 2001, which appeared in the online version of the SAN FRANCISCO CHRONICLE and is available in a letterpress broadside edition exclusively from the Fearless Books website: *www.fearlessbooks.com/HorseandWolf.html.*

———

Visit the Fearless Books website for more books, feature stories, reviews of titles from other independent publishers, and much more:

www.fearlessbooks.com